942.081

The Life and World of

MARY SEACOLE

Brian Williams

H www.heinemann/library.co.uk
Visit our website to find out more information about **Heinemann Library** books.

To order:
☎ Phone 44 (0) 1865 888066
▤ Send a fax to 44 (0) 1865 314091
▢ Visit the Heinemann Library Bookshop at www.heinemann/library.co.uk to browse our catalogue and order online.

First published in Great Britain by Heinemann Library, Halley Court, Jordan Hill, Oxford OX2 8EJ, part of Harcourt Education. Heinemann is a registered trademark of Harcourt Education Ltd.

Editorial: Lucy Thunder and Helen Cox
Design: Ron Kamen and Celia Floyd
Illustrations: Jeff Edwards and Joanna Brooker
Picture Research: Rebecca Sodergren and Elaine Willis
Production: Séverine Ribierre

Originated by Ambassador Litho Ltd
Printed in Hong Kong, China
by Wing King Tong

ISBN 0 431 14784 1
07 06 05 04 03
10 9 8 7 6 5 4 3 2 1

British Library Cataloguing in Publication Data
Williams, Brian
Life and world of Mary Seacole
610.7'3'092

A full catalogue record for this book is available from the British Library.

Acknowledgements
The publishers would like to thank the following for permission to reproduce photographs:
Amoret Tanner Collection p. **28**; Bodleian Library p. **27**; Bridgeman Art Library/Private Collection p. **4**; Bridgeman Art Library/Christie's Images p. **8**; Bridgeman Art Library/Guildhall Library, Corporation of London p. **9**; Bridgeman Art Library/Private Collection p. **10**; Bridgeman Art Library/The Forbes Magazine Collection, New York p. **11**; Bridgeman Art Library/Collection of the Earl of Pembroke, Wilton House, Wiltshire p. **16**; Bridgeman Art Library/Private Collection p. **17**; Bridgeman Art Library/The Stapleton Collection p. **20**; Bridgeman Art Library/Bridgeman Art Library/Musée de Beaux-Arts, Caen/Giraudon p.**22**; Corbis pp. **15** (Richard Hamilton-Smith), **23**; Florence Nightingale Museum p29; Fotomas pp. **12**, **21**; Illustrated London News p. **24**; Mary Evans Picture Library pp. **6**, **14**, **19**, **25**, **26**; National Trust p. **13**;

Cover photograph of Mary Seacole, reproduced with permission of the Florence Nightingale Museum.

The publishers would like to thank Rebecca Vickers for her assistance in the preparation of this book.

Every effort has been made to contact copyright holders of any material reproduced in this book. Any omissions will be rectified in subsequent printings if notice is given to the publishers.

Contents

Any words appearing in the text in bold, **like this**, are explained in the Glossary.

Nurses who went to war

Mary Seacole was a nurse and carer, who went to war in the 1850s. Her adventures took her far from home, the island of Jamaica in the Caribbean. She met members of the British royal family, and was cheered by thousands of people in London. She wrote a book about her life, telling how she helped soldiers during the **Crimean War**.

A woman who stood out

In Queen Victoria's Britain, Mary Seacole stood out because she was a woman working and travelling alone. Also, she had a black mother and a white father. In Britain, this made her unusual, at a time when there were few black people in the country. Mary called herself a Creole (someone of mixed origins) with 'good Scotch blood coursing in my veins'.

◀ **There are few pictures of Mary Seacole. This portrait of her, now in Jamaica's National Library, was painted before the Crimean War.**

Mary's wonderful adventures

Mary Seacole's own book, called the *Wonderful Adventures of Mrs Seacole*, published in 1857, tells us about her early life and her adventures in the Crimean War. Many of the quotations in this book come from Mary's book. Her later life, after she went to the Crimea, was also reported in British newspapers and magazines.

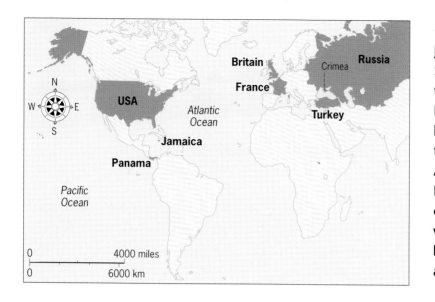

◄ This map shows Jamaica, where Mary Seacole was born. To the southwest is Panama, where she lived for a time. To the east, across the Atlantic Ocean, is Britain. Still further east is the Crimea, where Mary went to help British soldiers at war.

Mary Seacole made her own way in the world. She travelled to dangerous places, often risking her life, and earned her living as a businesswoman. She earned high praise from important people. Yet after she died in 1881, Mary Seacole was forgotten. Not until the mid-20th century did people 'rediscover' her brave work as a war nurse. Many saw her as a **role model**, a 19th-century independent woman.

Mrs Seacole and Miss Nightingale

The most famous nurse during the Crimean War was Florence Nightingale. She was English and was a trained nurse. She led a team of nurses to the **Crimea** and changed nursing for ever. Mrs Seacole was Jamaican and was not a trained nurse. She learned her medicine from her mother, and from doctors she watched at work. Unlike Florence Nightingale, she worked alone. Each of these remarkable women earned the affection and respect of the soldiers they helped.

Key dates

1805	Mary Jane Grant is born in Jamaica
1836	Mary marries Edwin Seacole
1837	Victoria is crowned queen
1850	Mary travels to Panama
1854	Mary sails for the Crimea to nurse British soldiers
1857	Mary's book is published
1881	Mary Seacole dies in London

Early days

What we know of Mary's early life comes from her own book. Her full name was Mary Jane Grant, and she was born in Kingston, Jamaica in 1805.

Mary's father was a Scottish soldier in the British Army. Her mother was a freed **slave**, of African origin, and ran a boarding house for invalid British soldiers and their families. Mary thought of herself as British. She enjoyed talking to British visitors to the house. Many islanders came, too, because Mary's mother was a 'doctress', a healer who made medicines.

Britain and Jamaica

Christopher Columbus had landed on Jamaica in 1494 and claimed the island for Spain. In 1655, British troops captured Jamaica from the Spanish, so when Mary was born the island had been a British **colony** for 150 years.

▲ Harbour Street in Kingston. This drawing was made in about 1835. The British flag flies over the town, and on the right a man and a soldier pass the time of day beside a water pump.

Jamaica in the early 1800s had a population of about 300,000. Of these, roughly 30,000 were white. Black Jamaicans were either slaves or freed slaves. Slaves worked on sugar **plantations**. Many freed slaves earned their living as coffee-growers, farmers, fishermen or shopkeepers.

Growing up busy

Mary was brought up by her mother and an old 'auntie'. As a little girl, she practised bandaging her doll, and gave medicines to cats and dogs, and herself. By the age of twelve Mary was helping her mother treat soldiers and their wives. She was always busy. As a grown-up, she later wrote 'I am sure I do not know what it is to be indolent [lazy]'.

▲ Many of the people of Jamaica worked on the island's sugar plantations. The sugar was made from sugar cane, a tall grass plant. The stalks of the cane were cut and then crushed to squeeze out the sugary juice.

Jamaica's slaves

The first people of Jamaica were Native Americans called Arawaks. Many were killed or made slaves by the Spanish. Others died of European diseases. To replace the Arawaks as slaves, the European settlers shipped in slaves from Africa to work on plantations. A British **Member of Parliament** named William Wilberforce led the fight against slavery. In 1807, Britain stopped the trade in slaves and in 1833 all slaves in the **British Empire** were officially freed.

A second home

Mary loved to look at the map, 'tracing the route to England', and to watch ships setting sail from Kingston. She longed to go to England, and as a teenager she got her wish, sailing with relatives for the port of Bristol. The travellers then took the **stagecoach** to London.

The Britain Mary saw

Mary loved London and stayed about a year, meeting members of her father's family. She knew quite a lot about Britain's history, about the wars with Napoleon Bonaparte's France, and Britain's two great war heroes, Admiral Horatio Nelson and the Duke of Wellington. The wars with France had ended in 1815, but old soldiers and sailors could still be seen. Some were limping beggars. Many were unable to find work in a fast-changing world. A new Britain was being hammered into shape by pounding steam engines in factories. The **Industrial Revolution** had begun.

▲ Mary landed at the seaport of Bristol, once a centre for the **slave** trade, then took a horse-drawn coach to London. The bumpy journey of 190 km took about 12 hours. Passengers rested at roadside inns, while fresh horses were harnessed to the coach.

Britain seemed a second home to Mary. On her next visit, she stayed for two years, visiting relatives and apparently paying her way by selling home-made pickles, as well as probably offering medical advice. Sailing back to Jamaica in 1825 was rather too exciting, for the ship caught fire. Fortunately, the fire was put out. Back home, Mary looked after her auntie until the old lady died, and then lived with her mother, helping her with her nursing. She loved to travel, and visited the Bahamas, Haiti and Cuba.

▶ The London that Mary explored on her first two visits was a city of around 1 million people – three times as many as on the whole of Jamaica. The streets were full of people, carts and carriages.

Britain steams ahead

Britain was the first country in the world to go through the Industrial Revolution. Changes had begun before Mary was born, with new machines being used in cotton mills and new steam engines powered by coal being developed. By 1820 Britain was fast becoming a nation of factories and factory workers. In 1819, when Mary was fourteen, steamships began crossing the English Channel. In 1830, the first steam railway started carrying passengers.

A short marriage

Like most 19th-century women, Mary expected to marry. She accepted a proposal of marriage from a man named Edwin Horatio Seacole, and they were married in 1836. In her book, Mary only calls him 'Mr Seacole'.

Making ends meet

The Seacoles opened a store in Jamaica. Edwin was not a healthy man and in spite of Mary's care, he died not long after their marriage, leaving her a **widow**. Soon afterwards her mother also died. 'It was no easy thing for a widow to make ends meet,' Mary later wrote in her book. She set to work with determination, earning 'not only my daily bread, but many comforts besides'.

She opened a boarding house of her own, and was kept busy caring for invalid army officers and their wives. She also sold pickles and preserves, made from local fruits and spices. Mary wrote in her book that one of her hardest struggles was to 'resist the pressing candidates for the late Mr Seacole's shoes' – meaning that other men wished to marry her. She was, after all, a successful businesswoman.

▲ Most of the houses in Kingston were wooden buildings. Mary called her boarding house the 'British Hotel'. Many of the city's buildings, including Mary's, burned down in 1843. This painting is a view of Kingston from 1838, before the fire.

A new queen and a new start

1837 was a year of celebrations. Jamaicans read in the newspapers about their new queen. The young Queen Victoria, only eighteen, had been crowned in London. People drank **toasts** to the new **Victorian age**.

In 1843, a terrible fire raged through Kingston. Many wooden houses went up in flames, and one of them was Mary's boarding house. She set to work getting it rebuilt. She was now a well-known figure among the British **garrison**, and knew many of the soldiers.

▼ When Victoria was crowned queen in 1837, she was queen not just of Britain but also of the **British Empire**. The Empire included small Caribbean islands like Jamaica.

A Victorian woman alone

In Victorian times, widows went into **mourning** for months after their husband's funeral, wearing black clothes. Queen Victoria wore black for 40 years after her husband, Prince Albert, died in 1861. Few women had well-paid jobs or money of their own, so most widows hoped to remarry. It was the only way they could afford to live.

Cholera strikes

Mary's skill as a nurse and 'doctress' was tested in 1850, by an outbreak of **cholera**. This was a deadly disease that spread wherever there were stinking drains and dirty drinking water. Doctors were only just realizing that cholera was caused by 'bad' drinking water. Cholera killed 62,000 people in London in 1848–49. By the 1860s, it was no longer a mass killer, because the city's sewers and water supply had been cleaned up.

Nursing the sick

The 1850 cholera outbreak in Jamaica killed 31,000 people. The islanders blamed dirty washing, sent ashore from an American ship in harbour. They pointed out that a washerwoman named Dolly Johnson was among the first victims.

Mary worked tirelessly to nurse the sick. She tried various treatments, comparing the results, and noting whether medicines worked or not. Making patients sick by giving them drinks of water and mustard seemed to help. She learned much by working alongside a British doctor, who was lodging in her house. Mary became sick herself. She was lucky. She caught a less serious form of cholera and recovered.

▶ This Victorian drawing shows how overcrowded parts of London were. In many places there was no clean water and toilets emptied into open drains and rivers. Diseases, such as cholera, spread quickly in conditions like this.

A change of scene

When she was well again, Mary decided on a change of scene. Her brother Edward Grant had gone to Panama in Central America. There he ran a hotel and store, selling goods to men on their way to the **goldfields** of California. Panama is on the narrow neck of land joining North and South America. In Mary's day, the jungles of Panama offered a short land crossing for travellers on their way to California. This saved them a long, stormy sea voyage around the tip of South America. Mary set off to help her brother, leaving a cousin in charge of her own business. She was in for a shock.

▶ This is a doctor's medical cabinet from the early 19th century. Mary would have known some of the medicines. Missing are modern **antibiotic drugs**, which were not used before the 1940s.

Fighting cholera

Cholera killed millions of people around the world during the 1800s. By the 1850s some medical experts had worked out that dirty drinking water could be the cause of the disease. **Bacteria** had been first seen under a microscope as early as the 1600s, but no one knew what they were. In the 1870s, Louis Pasteur of France and Robert Koch of Germany showed that certain bacteria caused diseases, such as cholera.

Nurse on her travels

Mary set off for Panama with her servant Mac, and many packages. She was hardly dressed for a mosquito-ridden tropical jungle, as she wore 'a delicate light blue dress, a white bonnet prettily trimmed and a shawl'. She travelled by river steamboat and then on a new railway through country she thought 'unhealthy and wretched'. The journey continued by boat up a river to the town of Cruces. Here she found her brother, in a town full of rough men (and some women) on their way to dig for gold in California.

◄ This is a drawing of travellers in trouble crossing Panama in 1849. People hired **mules** or porters to carry their belongings. There were no roads and lots of biting insects – and mishaps!

Nursing in Panama

Edward's 'Independent Hotel' was a log hut. Diners ate meals of pancakes, pork, dumplings, rice and **molasses** at a long table. Almost as soon as Mary arrived, she was nursing more **cholera** victims. There was no doctor, yet some men were at first reluctant to be treated by a woman. When a baby died despite her care, she carried out an **autopsy** on the body, to improve her medical knowledge.

▲ Panama has very dense forests. Even today, the country is not easy to travel through.

The new British Hotel

Mary opened her own 'British Hotel' opposite her brother's. She fed 50 men at her table and hired a barber to cut hair and shave beards. Eggs were so expensive that diners were charged by the number of shells left on their plates! She caught one American trying to hide his shells under the table.

Mary did not like Panama. There were frequent fights and murders, and too many strange things to eat. She shuddered at serving up iguanas, parrots and, worst of all, roast monkeys. She was not sorry to return to Jamaica in 1853.

Back home, Mary was called on to nurse victims of **yellow fever**. Many died. A young English surgeon died in her arms, and she kept a gold brooch with a lock of his hair, sent to her by his mother. On her last trip to Panama, she met Thomas Day, a mine manager and distant relative. He would join her in an even more dangerous adventure.

Black and white in the USA

In Panama, Mary was shocked by the **racism** of some Americans. Many thousands of blacks in the **Southern states** were **slaves**. White Southerners took this for granted. Most people in the Northern states thought slavery was wrong. A book published in 1852, called *Uncle Tom's Cabin*, about a black slave, added to the arguments about slavery. The split between North and South over slavery led to the American Civil War in 1861.

War news

In 1854, news reached Jamaica of war in Europe. On her old map, Mary marked with a cross an unfamiliar name: the **Crimea**, a distant corner of the Russian **Empire**.

The soldiers depart

Ships left Kingston crammed with soldiers on their way to war. Mary wanted to go, too, to offer medical care. Old soldiers had told her of the terrible injuries caused by **musket** balls and exploding cannon shot. Rotten food, filth and disease would kill as many men as the Russians. She packed and took ship for England.

▲ Britain's war minister, Sidney Herbert (1810–61), did not accept Mary Seacole's offer of help because he had no idea who she was.

Soon after the first big Crimean battle, at the Alma River in September 1854, Mary was in London. Reports came in of two more battles, at Balaclava (25 October) and Inkermann (5 November). Army hospitals were filled with wounded and dying men. Nurses were needed desperately. In November 1854, a storm wrecked many ships carrying vital supplies to the Crimea. The soldiers faced a miserable winter.

Mary goes it alone

Mary wrote to the War Minister, Sir Sidney Herbert. Neither he nor his wife, who was helping to arrange for women nurses to go to the Crimea, would see her. She met a friend of Florence Nightingale, who was to lead the nurses, but was told that no more nurses were needed. Mary later wondered if her 'duskier skin' had something to do with her rejection. Yet she did not blame anyone. She had letters from her old army friends, but few people in London knew her.

Mary decided to make her own way to the Crimea. She met up again with Thomas Day, and they agreed to become partners, 'to establish a mess table and comfortable quarters for sick and convalescent officers'. In January 1855, Mary Seacole sailed off to war, determined to be 'the right woman in the right place'.

▲ This is one of the earliest war photographs. It shows a British army camp in the Crimea and was taken by the **pioneer** photographer Roger Fenton.

The Crimean War

Britain and France feared Russia was trying to enlarge its Empire, by making war in 1853 on the Ottoman Empire (which included modern-day Turkey). To help the Turks defeat the Russians, the British and French sent ships to the Crimea, to land troops. The soldiers arrived in September 1854. The **Crimean War** was the first big war reported by newspaper reporters and photographers. It ended in 1856.

In the Crimea

Mary enjoyed the long sea voyage to the **Crimea** 'amazingly'. She stopped off at the Rock of Gibraltar on the way. Here she met two soldier-friends, wounded in the Crimea and on their way home. They told her how awful things were: hot in summer, cold in winter, dirt everywhere, no proper clothing, food or medicines.

Arriving in Turkey

Letters from Thomas Day, already in the Crimea, told Mary what supplies she should buy in Turkey. As soon as her ship anchored at Constantinople (now Istanbul), Mary crossed by small boat to the town of Scutari. Here Florence Nightingale and her nurses had turned an old Turkish army building into a hospital. Mary met Miss Nightingale, busily setting the hospital to rights and demanding more help from the army.

To the front line

Mary was determined to reach the battlefield. With her supplies, she sailed for Balaclava. There she landed her stores, spending the nights on an **ammunition ship** in the harbour. She slept on top of barrels filled with gunpowder, making sure that all candles and lamps were safely out before bedtime!

▶ This map shows the Crimean peninsula (a peninsula is a piece of land almost surrounded by sea). Marked on it are the main battlefields and Scutari, where the main army hospital was.

▲ This picture shows British and French ships crowded into the harbour at Balaclava. For a time, Mary slept on board a ship – it was safer than being on land.

Mary was soon busy, helping the army doctors. Sick and wounded men were brought from the battles in carts used as 'ambulances' (a word used for the first time in English). She did what she could to help them. As well as cleaning and bandaging their wounds, she baked sponge cakes and handed out cool drinks of lemonade.

The lady with the lamp

Florence Nightingale (1820–1910) was fifteen years younger than Mary Seacole. She had studied nursing in Germany, against the wishes of her family. In 1854 she went to Turkey with 38 other women to nurse the soldiers wounded in the fighting. Watching her walk through the hospital rooms at night, the men called her 'the lady with the lamp'. She ended up being put in charge of all British Army hospitals in the Crimea.

Mrs Seacole's store

Mary's **Crimean** 'British Hotel' outside Balaclava was named Spring Hill. There was a shop, storeroom, kitchen and restaurant. Upstairs was her little hospital. There were private rooms for Mary, Thomas Day and their servants. Mary hired Turkish workers.

Thieves, rats and good food

Mary had four horse-drawn carts to carry her supplies from the harbour to Spring Hill. She was troubled by thieves who stole her food, and the rats, she wrote, were as bad as 'hungry schoolboys'. However, there were worse perils. After Mary's washerwoman was murdered, Thomas Day gave her a gun to defend herself.

Soldiers came for decent food and 'sick comforts'. The soldiers paid what they could, and Mary spent the money on more food, blankets and medicines.

▲ The road from Balaclava to the British Army camp passed by Mary's British Hotel. As this picture shows, it was usually crowded with carts being pulled by oxen, horses and mules.

The daily round

Every day, Mary would roast 20 or more chickens and bake hams. Her precious stores included tinned soup and meat, tinned salmon and oysters, butter, sardines, tobacco, tea, coffee and tooth powder. Fresh vegetables and eggs were a rare treat. Even a visiting French **chef** named Alexis Soyer, sent to see how bad army food was, liked the look and tastes of Mary's restaurant.

▲ Mary Seacole in her British Hotel greets the French chef, Alexis Soyer. He was impressed by her tireless work looking after the soldiers. The two became friends.

Mary was usually up and busy by 5 a.m. Hot coffee, with sugar and butter (no milk) was served to the soldiers at 7 a.m. She cared for the sick and wounded until noon. In the afternoon she sold clothing, saddles, boots and shoes. At 8 p.m. 'the curtain descended on that day's labour'.

Soldiers in the Crimea

Soldiers in the Crimea were expected to find their own food, either buying it from a storekeeper or stealing it from somebody else. The army made little attempt to feed, clothe or nurse its men. It expected them to fight, obey orders and look after themselves. Small towns sprang up around the camps where the soldiers lived in tents and huts. Some officers had their wives living with them.

On the battlefield

In the **Crimea**, battles were watched by onlookers. Spectators, including officers' wives, rode out to peer through the gunsmoke from hilltops. Mary handed out food and drinks to soldiers as they marched off in lines. She followed on horseback, with two **mules** carrying her medical supplies. Often she had to ride through bursting **shells** from Russian **cannons**, and iron cannon balls which ploughed up the ground 'more frequently than was agreeable'.

The confusion of war

Crimean battles were very confused. Infantry soldiers marched on foot, in long lines or columns. Cavalry galloped around on horses. More horses hauled the heavy cannons on wheels into position. As battle raged, neither side could see what was happening through clouds of smoke from the roaring guns. Some wounded soldiers were left to die where they fell. Those who were carried back to camp often died of infections or shock, as shattered arms and legs were **amputated** without **anaesthetic**. Many men died because they were exhausted, hungry, cold and sick.

▼ **An artist's view of the battle of Sebastopol in 1855.**

Mary watches battles

In August 1855, Mary stood looking down on a battle as Russian troops were driven back. Afterwards she walked around, helping to nurse the wounded and dying.

In September, she watched the British and French attacks on the Russian town of Sebastopol. The fighting was very fierce. The French captured a fort, but the British were driven back. Many British soldiers were killed and wounded. The weary Russians withdrew, however. Mary was the first woman into the still-burning town. She gave out refreshments and bandaged the wounded.

Soldiers offered her presents of sofas and chairs, taken from Russian houses. She accepted a cracked teapot, a **parasol** and a bell. Later she used the bell to knock off the cap of a French soldier, who tried to arrest her as an enemy spy!

▶ **William Howard Russell (1820–1907) was** *The Times* **newspaper's special correspondent in the Crimea. His description of British soldiers at the battle of Balaclava as the 'thin red line' became famous.**

War news

While watching the attack on Sebastopol, Mary Seacole met William H. Russell. He was Britain's first famous war reporter. Every day he **telegraphed** reports of the fighting to London, to be printed in *The Times* newspaper. His descriptions of the war, of the lack of supplies and the sufferings of the soldiers, shocked readers back home in Britain. Russell became Mary's friend, calling her in one of his articles 'a kind and successful physician'.

Returning heroes

After the battle of Sebastopol, the Russians had had enough. Though neither side had 'won', the shooting stopped. The soldiers relaxed. They enjoyed picnics, cricket matches, horse races and shows. At Christmas, everyone ate 'Aunty Seacole's plum pudding' and mince pies. Mary dined on wild bustard (a turkey-like bird).

Now that it was safer to travel, Mary went on sightseeing trips. She explored the hills and valleys of the **Crimea**, and met her first Russians. She also visited the war cemeteries, planting lilac trees and shrubs around the freshly dug graves.

Homecoming

Early in 1856, the troops began packing to go home. Many came to say goodbye and thank you to Mary. However, peace brought her problems. The British Hotel still had piles of stores, which she could no longer sell. Mary closed the hotel, and sold what she could, but for a tenth of its old value.

Mary returned to England, poorer than when she had left. Thomas Day said farewell; he decided to try his luck in Australia. Mary had come home with letters of thanks from patients and friends. Lord William Painter, a senior army officer, wrote in July 1856 that she had carried on her work 'even in positions of great danger'. But such letters would not pay her bills.

▶ This picture, published in the magazine *Illustrated London News*, shows Mary Seacole saying her goodbyes to troops in the Crimea.

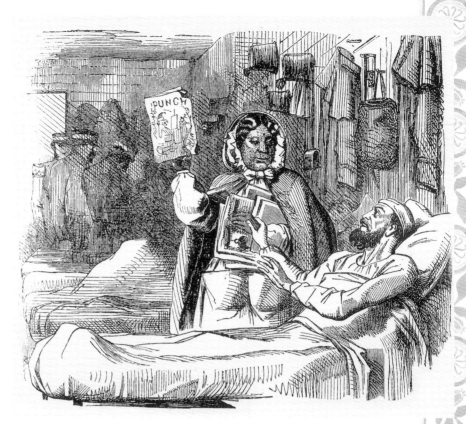

▶ *Punch* was a popular humorous magazine. It often poked fun at politicians in cartoons and funny verses. But it also praised heroes. Mary Seacole was turned into a celebrity by *Punch*'s support for her bravery in the Crimea.

Starting again

Back in England, Mary opened a new store in the army town of Aldershot, but it was a failure. She moved back to London. Now she had no money left, and in November 1856 she faced charges of **bankruptcy**.

Her friends rallied round to help. A writer to *The Times* newspaper asked: 'While the deeds of Florence Nightingale are being handed down to posterity [later generations] are the actions of Mrs Seacole to be entirely forgotten?' The magazine *Punch* published a poem in her honour. It was called 'A Stir for Seacole'. It ended with an appeal: 'What red-coat [British soldier] in all the land, But to set her upon her legs again, Will not lend a willing hand?'

The new Britain

The Britain Mary came back to was changing. The Great Exhibition of 1851 had shown off all kinds of new machines and inventions. Britain had become the 'workshop of the world'. Yet many of the men coming home from the **Crimean War** found only hardship. Some ex-soldiers got jobs on farms, in mines and factories, or on the new railways. Crippled men had little hope of a job. Many ended up selling their medals won for bravery.

Wonderful adventures end

Mary's friends raised money to help her get back on her feet. In *The Times* of April 1857, William Howard Russell told readers how he had seen Mary Seacole taking her comforts to wounded men, under fire. 'A more tender or skilful hand about a wound or broken limb could not be found among our best surgeons,' he wrote.

Mary writes a book and takes a bow

Soldiers' books about the **Crimean War** were selling well. So, in 1857, Mary wrote her own life story. Her book was called *Wonderful Adventures of Mrs Seacole in many lands*. It sold well. Twenty thousand people came to a concert held to raise money for her. *The Times* reported that when the audience shouted Mary's name, 'the genial [kindly] old lady rose ... and smiled'.

1857 was the year of the **Indian Mutiny**. Mary wanted to go to India, to help the army again. It was said that Queen Victoria herself said 'no'. Mrs Seacole must not risk her life again.

▲ **This painting shows Queen Victoria with soldiers who had fought in the Crimean War.**

Later years

Though seldom seen in public, Mary Seacole was not forgotten. In 1867, another fund to help her was supported by the Prince of Wales. In the early 1870s, the Princess of Wales asked Mary to give her massage treatment for lameness. In London streets, Mary was frequently greeted by old soldiers.

The 1881 **census** listed Mrs Mary Seacole as resident at 3 Cambridge Street, Paddington, London. On 14 May 1881, she died and her death was reported in the newspapers. Mary may have had a daughter – a friend, the **chef** Alexis Soyer, wrote of meeting 'Sarah Seacole'. However, Mary did not mention any child in her book. She was buried in Kensal Rise Cemetery, London. Her tombstone inscription called her 'a notable nurse'.

WONDERFUL ADVENTURES of Mrs SEACOLE

LONDON
JAMES BLACKWOOD
PATERNOSTER ROW

▶ This is the front cover of Mary Seacole's book, which became a bestseller in 1857. The newspaper reporter William Howard Russell wrote an introduction to the book, which he called 'unique in literature'.

Nursing becomes a profession

Before the Crimean War, nursing was thought of as a job fit only for poor, ignorant women. Britain had no trained nurses. The work of Florence Nightingale and Mary Seacole changed the way people thought about nursing for ever. Britain's first training school for nurses was founded in 1860 at St Thomas's Hospital in London.

A notable nurse

Mary's book tells us all we know about her early life. In his introduction to the book, William Howard Russell called her 'a plain truth-speaking woman' and hoped that 'England will not forget one who nursed her sick'.

Forgotten until the 1950s

Unfortunately, like many heroes, Mary was forgotten once her friends had died. Few people, in or outside of nursing, had heard of Mary Seacole. Then, in 1954, one hundred years after she left Jamaica for the **Crimean War**, Jamaican nurses renamed their headquarters building Mary Seacole House. The University of the West Indies also named a students' hall of residence after her.

In 1973 Mary Seacole's grave in London was restored, and in 1981 the 100th anniversary of her death was marked by a memorial service. Her book was reprinted in 1984. More people wanted to know about this remarkable woman.

▶ Nurses today can look to Mary Seacole as a **role model**. She was never afraid of danger, and went wherever she knew her work was needed.

Why is Mary Seacole remarkable?

Mary Seacole's life is interesting in many ways. Her book is one of the few books by a Caribbean-born woman in the 19th century. Her adventures took her from the Caribbean to Britain, a journey later made by thousands of other people, as **immigrants** in the 1950s. She made her own way in the world, not easy for a woman of mixed race and a **widow**. In the **Victorian age**, few women travelled to such rough and dangerous places, or lived and worked among men on equal terms. In her book, Mary gives her own fresh view of the Victorian world. She mixed with people of all kinds. The people she met admired her courage, honesty and kindness.

As a **pioneer** 'nurse practioner', Mary Seacole carried out many treatments usually done only by doctors. Her practical nursing saved many lives. Her techniques included traditional medicines and common sense – such as keeping patients clean, warm and well fed. She is now honoured with a leadership award given to nurses by the British Department of Health. Florence Nightingale is remembered as the founder of modern nursing. Mary Seacole, who worked alone to help others, was an inspiring pioneer, too, through her 'wonderful adventures'.

▶ This bust of Mary Seacole was made in 1871 by one of her old army patients, Count Gleichen (a relative of Queen Victoria). It shows her wearing medals given to her by Britain, France and Turkey for her work in the Crimean War.

Glossary

ammunition ship ship loaded with gunpowder, bullets and weapons

amputated body part cut off by a surgeon in a hospital

anaesthetic pain-killer used by doctors

antibiotic drugs germ-killing medicines, invented in the mid-20th century

autopsy studying the inside of a body by cutting it open

bacteria tiny, microscopic germs that can cause disease

bankruptcy failure in business

British Empire countries ruled by Britain or linked to it. By 1880 over 370 million people lived in the Empire.

cannon big gun on wheels, which fired solid balls or exploding shells

census a count and survey of all the people in a country

chef cook, in a hotel or restaurant

cholera disease causing sickness and diarrhoea

colony territory ruled or settled by people from another country

Crimea area of land almost surrounded by the Black Sea, now part of Ukraine

Crimean War war of 1853–56; Britain, France and Turkey fought against Russia

empire several countries, all ruled by one person or government

garrison soldiers guarding a fort or base

goldfield area where miners search for gold

immigrant person moving from one country to another, to make a new life

Indian Mutiny uprising in 1857 among Indian soldiers against British rule

Industrial Revolution period of history (early 19th century) when machines and steam power were used to make things more quickly

Member of Parliament person elected to the House of Commons

molasses thick treacle made from sugar

mourning time of sadness after someone has died

mule a cross between a horse and a donkey

musket weapon like a rifle, firing one shot at a time

mutton meat from adult sheep

parasol sunshade, like an umbrella

pioneer someone who is one of the first to do something

plantation big farm where one crop (such as sugar or coffee) is grown

racism unfair treatment of people because of their race or skin colour

role model someone who is an example to others

shell metal case fired from a cannon, which explodes violently

slave servant or worker owned by another person

Southern states parts of the USA that supported slavery and fought the Northern states in the American Civil War (1861–65)

stagecoach passenger-carrying vehicle pulled by horses

telegraph system for sending messages in code electrically through wires

toast drinking the health of someone, at a dinner or party, to wish them well

Victorian age time of Queen Victoria's reign, 1837–1901

widow woman whose husband has died

yellow fever tropical disease spread by mosquito bites

Timeline

1805	Mary Jane Grant is born in Jamaica
1815	Napoleon Bonaparte is defeated by the British and Prussians at the Battle of Waterloo
1825	Mary returns to Jamaica after her second visit to Britain
1830	Britain has the world's first steam passenger railway
1833	All slaves in the British Empire are freed by a new law
1836	Mary marries Edwin Seacole
1837	Victoria is crowned queen
1843	Mary's hotel in Kingston is burned down
1850	Mary travels to Panama
1851	The Great Exhibition of arts and sciences is held in London
1854	Mary sails for the Crimea to nurse British soldiers fighting there
1856	The Crimean War ends
1857	Mary's book is published. She is stopped from going to India.
1860	Florence Nightingale starts Britain's first training school for nurses
1867	A second fund is launched to raise money for Mary
1881	Mary Seacole dies in London

Further reading & websites

Mary Seacole; a story from the Crimean War, Sam Godwin (Hodder Wayland, 2001)
Mary Seacole, John Malam (Evans, 1999)
Wonderful Adventures of Mrs Seacole in many lands, Mary Seacole's own book (The X Press, 1999)

Heinemann Explore – an online resource from Heinemann. For Key Stage 2 history go to *www.heinemannexplore.co.uk*

www.maryseacole.com – website of the Mary Seacole Centre

www.learnaboutnursing.org – website all about nursing

Places to visit

Imperial War Museum, London
Imperial War Museum North, Salford Quays, Manchester
National Army Museum, London
National Portrait Gallery, London

Index

Titles in the *Life and World Of* series include:

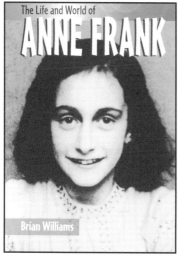

The Life and World of
ANNE FRANK
Brian Williams

Hardback   0 431 14780 9

The Life and World of
ELIZABETH I
Struan Reid

Hardback   0 431 14781 7

The Life and World of
FLORENCE NIGHTINGALE
Struan Reid

Hardback   0 431 14782 5

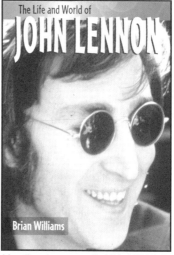

The Life and World of
JOHN LENNON
Brian Williams

Hardback   0 431 14783 3

The Life and World of
MARY SEACOLE
Brian Williams

Hardback   0 431 14784 1

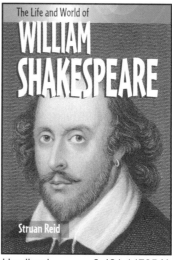

The Life and World of
WILLIAM SHAKESPEARE
Struan Reid

Hardback   0 431 14785 X

Find out about the other titles in this series on our website www.heinemann.co.uk/library